# COSTUME OF THE
# CLASSICAL WORLD

# COSTUME OF THE CLASSICAL WORLD

## MARION SICHEL

# BATSFORD ACADEMIC AND EDUCATIONAL LTD

First published 1980
Reprinted 1984
© Marion Sichel 1980

Printed and bound in Great Britain by
Anchor Brendon Ltd, Tiptree, Essex
for the Publishers
Batsford Academic and Education Limited
4 Fitzhardinge Street London W1H 0AH

ISBN 0 7134 1511 8

# _____ CONTENTS _____

Classical in its strictest sense means 'Greek and Roman' but the 'Classical world' has come to include not only Greece and Italy but Egypt, the Bible lands, Ethiopia, Assyria, Babylon and Persia: all the civilisations, in fact, which flourished between 3000 BC and the fifth century AD and which at one time or another came into contact with the Greeks, or fell under the sway of the Roman Empire. This book shows the costume of all these early peoples.

It is important to remember that the civilisations of the Classical world flourished at different times. When Egyptian dress had reached its fully evolved form the people of Ancient Britain were still dressed in animal skins. Through trade, war and conquest different cultures came into contact with each other, and influenced one another's costume. For example, the Romans introduced their tunics and cloaks into Gaul, but also adopted from the Gauls the idea of wearing breeches for fighting in cold climates.

Apart from the obvious differences in appearance, there are some striking differences between ancient and modern dress. Firstly, there were none of the rapid changes in fashion that we experience today. Even in the days of the late Roman Empire, changes were relatively slow to occur. Secondly, dress had a symbolic value in ancient times: rank and authority showed in the costumes worn. Higher ranks were seen wearing better quality and greater amounts of material which was also more colourful. The lower ranks and the poor wore fewer and less elaborate garments. The wealthier the person, the more the clothing worn. Thus a wealthy person would wear not only a loincloth or underskirt but also a tunic on top. Finally, clothing was usually homespun, and often the same piece of cloth could serve as a garment, a blanket or a shroud.

The first evidence for clothing generally dates from about 3000 BC, when it consisted of two types of garment. One was a loin-cloth of sheepskin, fastened around the waist with a belt. The other also consisted of a loincloth, but with the loose ends pulled up between the thighs. Thus an open and a closed garment emerged, which could be worn either together or separately.

A great deal is known about Ancient Egyptian costume as a large amount of reference material is preserved in tombs in the form of ornaments, statues and wall paintings. In the very early times the slaves and poorer people were naked, whilst the wealthier wore a loincloth, and then a development from this, the tunic, which was, in effect, a loincloth extended down and lengthened upwards to the shoulders, fastening with a pin. Over the years, clothes became more complex: collars were added for decoration and the tunic could be fringed. On the whole, however, changes in costume occurred gradually and infrequently over the Egyptian period, and this is perhaps a reflection of the stability of these early times. The Egyptians retained their typical costumes until Roman times.

It is the resemblance rather than the disparities in Greek and Roman styles of dress which are apparent. Similarities in costume are to be expected because of the close contact between the two civilisations. Greeks settled in southern Italy in the sixth century BC and later on Greece was incorporated into the Roman Empire for several centuries, the citizens of Greek towns eventually becoming citizens of Rome. The principal aspects of Greek costume were thus adopted by the Romans. Greece was to the late Romans what Paris was to eighteenth and nineteenth century Europe — a source of art and fashion. In both Greek and Roman costume clothes were loose and free — at no other time in history have such practical as well as graceful garments been fashionable. Lengths of material of varying sizes and shapes were draped around the body rather than fitting it closely, and were fastened with girdles and pins.

Linen and woollen garments were in use among the early Egyptians at the time of the Pharaohs. Linen especially was an important export from Egypt and much of the yarn was made up in Jerusalem. It was frequently used as a garment lining as it was finer and softer in texture than wool. Wool and linen could be intermixed in the making of material, a practice which probably originated with the Egyptians. Cotton was also manufactured at a very early date, but silk was not introduced into Egypt until much later.

The art of tanning and dressing leather was a skill possessed by the ancient Egyptians. The earliest garments were made of animal skins and leather was worn extensively, even when cloth was in use. Shoes and girdles were generally made of leather.

The art of dyeing materials was known from a very early period, as was embroidery, and the embroidery in the later Egyptian periods was sumptuous, gold thread made of beaten and rounded strips of metal being used. Much of the embroidery was so fine that it could be taken for painting.

For over 3000 years the Egyptian style of dress altered only gradually. The basic and earliest garment worn by men of the Old

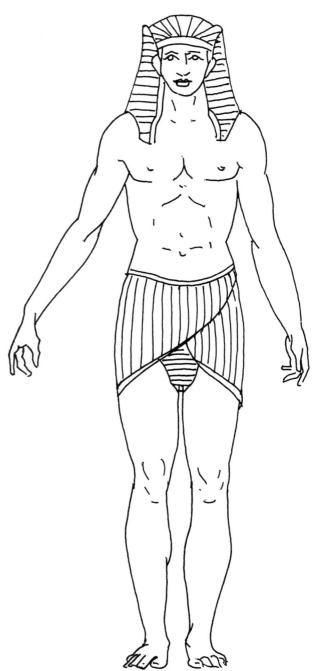

*Schenti worn by Egyptian man with cloth head covering*

Simple Egyptian costume. The false black hair was
made of wool

A kalasiris with an embroidered hem and two wide
straps over the shoulders is shown here. The pectoral
around the neck is smaller than that of a man

Kingdom (*c* 3000 BC) was the loincloth or schenti which was wrapped around the body several times and kept in place by a girdle. The schenti was made of linen for the Pharaohs and priests, the common people wearing it in leather or woven vegetable fibres. The wealthier people had their loincloths enriched with gold thread and the important wore them pleated and stiffened into a triangular apron. The quality of the material and the amount of drapery was the only distinguishing factor between the noble- and the lower classes. Women in this period wore sheath-like, tight-fitting dresses. Deep collars, decorated with embroidery and beads, were introduced at an early date, and worn by men and women.

Costume evolved slowly during the years of the Middle Kingdom (2200-1800 BC). Men began to wear linen capes with the schenti, knotted on the breast.

After the establishment of the New Kingdom *c* 1500 BC the kalasiris, worn by both men and women, was common. This was a kind of tunic made of a transparent linen gauze with a design at the base and was worn over a loincloth.

There were several types of kalasiris, some with sleeves. In its simplest form the garment consisted of a rectangular piece of material with a hole in the centre, through which the head could be inserted. The sides were sewn together, leaving space for the arms to pass through. When sleeves were present these were made separately and sewn on. The kalasiris might cover the body with a band over one shoulder, or it might reach up to the neck. It could be sleeveless or have either short and narrow or long and wide sleeves. The body of the kalasiris also varied in width, being either full and wide, or so close-fitting that movement was very restricted. The materials used were either woven or knitted, allowing for a certain amount of elasticity when it was made in one piece. Another style was short and resembled a

◄ *Egyptian woman in a simple garment of thin material*

woman's petticoat. The kalasiris was generally worn with a girdle around the waist. If no girdle was worn, the rectangular shape was slightly modified so that it narrowed at the shoulders. Working people wore the kalasiris shorter and tucked up to allow for greater freedom of movement.

Egyptian women wore the kalasiris or tunic on its own, but their garments were more ornately embroidered than those worn by the men. Their clothes were very often of a transparent material pleated in a type of sunray pleating. Queen Nefertiti (c 1390-1354 BC), for example, often wore a long tight dress over which was a pleated tunic with wide batwing sleeves; this was belted just under the bosom. A wide collar consisting of many necklaces was also fashionable. Necklines were generally quite low and the shoulder straps of the tunics became wide. Later it became fashionable to have just one shoulder strap, leaving the other shoulder bare. All colours were popular except black, which was reserved for wigs.

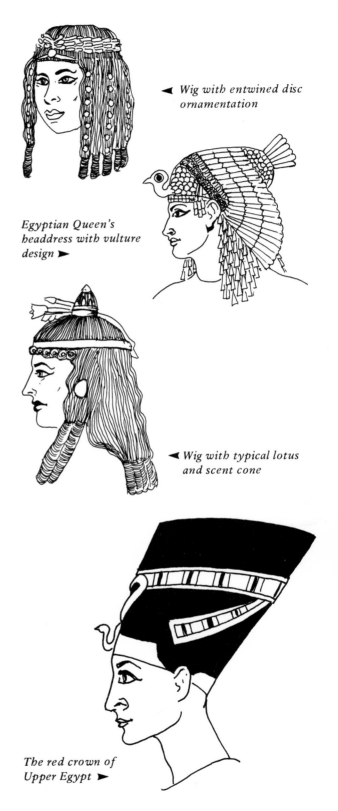

◀ *Wig with entwined disc ornamentation*

*Egyptian Queen's headdress with vulture design* ▶

◀ *Wig with typical lotus and scent cone*

## HAIRSTYLES

Noblemen had shaven heads and no beards, hair only being allowed to grow in times of mourning or while travelling. Boys also had their heads shaven, except for one lock of hair at the side.

Wigs were a basic item of Egyptian attire for both men and women. They were made of real hair, flax, or wool made into plaits or locks and were black in colour. The poor had often to be satisfied with wigs in felt. Men's wigs were usually in a round shape, following the contours of the head. The hair was often fairly short just covering the ears, but shoulder length wigs were also worn.

Generally, women wore their wigs long, although they did sometimes imitate men's hairstyles. Hair ornamentation using braiding, jewels and flowers was very popular. The lotus was especially favoured as it was the symbol of Egypt.

*The red crown of Upper Egypt* ▶

10

*Short Egyptian wig
with diadem ornamen-
◄ tation*

*Long woollen Egyptian
wig with cloth head
covering ►*

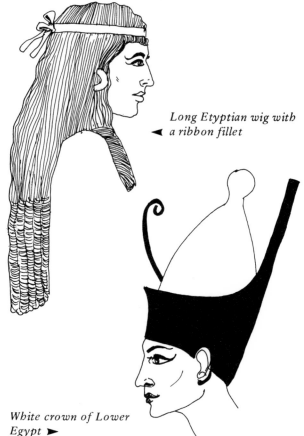

*Long Etyptian wig with
◄ a ribbon fillet*

*White crown of Lower
Egypt ►*

For ceremonial occasions false beards, perfumed and curled, were worn by men. Like the wigs, they were made of false hair and ended in an upturned point.

## HEADWEAR

Head coverings varied with changes in fashion and according to the wealth and rank of the owner. Sovereigns and divinities are shown wearing various types of complex headdress, including a kind of mitre which was high-crowned with a boss on top. Some styles had ornamenta borders and resembled night caps, while others had horn-like radiations. The crown of Upper Egypt was a tall white crown with plumes, or a design showing a sun disc. There was also a striped linen headcloth, called a klaft, which King Tutankhamun is shown wearing. The material covered the brow and hung down on either side of the face. This was a royal headdress.

Around 1400 BC it became fashionable to have an elongated head shape and so, to enhance the profile, it was common practice to polish the head. The most fashionable men and women often placed on top of their head cones of scented grease, which slowly melted over their head and shoulders, making the skin oily and glistening.

## FOOTWEAR

At first only priests wore foot coverings; these were in the form of sandals with leather, papyrus or wooden soles held on by straps. Later these began to be worn more generally. Footwear, when worn, was the same for both men and women. It consisted of simple open sandals made either of leather or papyrus, held on with a thong between the large and second toe and a strap over the top of the foot. For ceremonial occasions the sandals were made more elaborate with jewelled ornamentation.

*11*

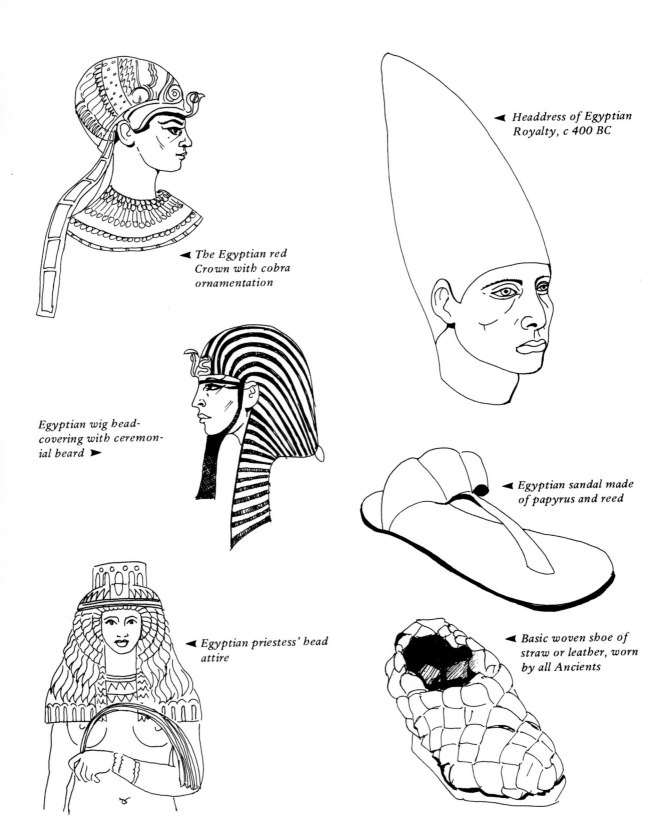

◄ The Egyptian red Crown with cobra ornamentation

◄ Headdress of Egyptian Royalty, c 400 BC

Egyptian wig head-covering with ceremonial beard ►

◄ Egyptian sandal made of papyrus and reed

◄ Egyptian priestess' head attire

◄ Basic woven shoe of straw or leather, worn by all Ancients

## CHILDREN

Children wore the same clothes as their parents or else they went naked.

## JEWELLERY

Ornamental jewellery was worn from a very early period and the Egyptians, both men and women, wore rings and chains as well as beads, necklaces and bracelets, which were worn not only on the arms but as leg oranmentation as well. Earrings were also in evidence and diadems or circlets of gold were worn on the head. Gold was one of the favourite metals used. Glass was also utilised, coloured blue, green, purple, red, etc, in the form of trinkets and beads that could be made into necklaces, bracelets and earrings.

A favourite neck ornament with all ranks and both men and women, was the pectoral which generally consisted of a gold plaque, suspended at chest level on a decorated chain. The pectoral was semi-circular or rectangular and was adorned with rows of ornamentation. Pectorals for the wealthy might be set with precious stones. Those worn by women would be smaller than the men's.

## MAKE-UP AND ACCESSORIES

Pumice stone was used extensively on the knees and elbows to keep them soft, and also to remove excess hair.

Make-up was very important for women. It was fashionable to use a foundation made of white lead paste. The lips were coloured

*The pectoral consisted of many rows of ornamental work and was very colourful: red, blue, black and white in sequence*

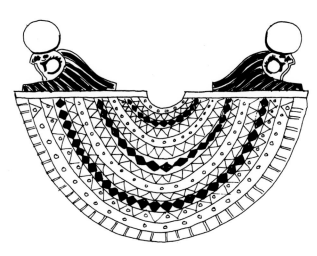

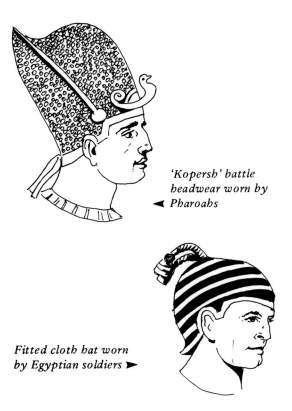

*'Kopersh' battle headwear worn by* ◄ *Pharoahs*

*Fitted cloth hat worn by Egyptian soldiers* ►

13

with an orange colouring, a precise outline being achieved with a small brush, and the same colour was used on the cheeks from the cheekbones towards the temples. Eye make-up was especially important, the eyes being lengthened and accentuated by a black kohl line and shaded on the lids with a green powder, while the eyebrows were lengthened with a greyish powder so that they arched towards the cheeks. Toenails and fingernails were lacquered to make them shiny.

Combs and hairpins were made of ivory, metal or wood. Mirrors, either circular or oval in shape, were of highly polished bronze or ivory. Umbrellas and fans originated in Egypt and were either long handled (to be carried by slaves) or shorter handled (designed to be carried by the individual).

## MILITARY AND CLERGY

Military uniform was very similar to civilian wear, consisting of a loincloth or skirt and a leather apron and breastplate. Egyptian armour consisted of a pectoral or breast-plate (this was also adopted by Persian warriors), made of linen which was folded and plaited in such a way that it was able to resist weapons. The usual weapons were short swords, bucklers and javelins. Egyptian sailors wore quilted helmets and had convex shields, javelins and double-edged axes.

Egyptian priests wore pleated linen skirts, and sometimes a leopard skin on top. They had their heads shaven and wore high-crowned caps with an asp or serpent wreath.

# ETHIOPIA

raw ox hide shields and arrows whose heads were made of sharp stones. Their javelins were of sharpened goat's horn. In battle they painted the top half of their body with a kind of white plaster and the remainder with vermilion dye.

*An Ethiopian noble lady*

The Ethiopians' original dress was a simple wool or leather loincloth with a cloak-like garment over it. They dressed, in fact, in much the same way as the Egyptians whose country was just north of Ethiopia, but as their civilisation evolved their style of dress became more Asiatic or Assyrian. The loincloth was later worn only by the upper classes for ceremonial occasions: for everyday wear long garments were worn.

The materials used were opaque. Both men and women wore a long, rectangular cloth that reached from the chest to the ground; this was draped around the body and fastened at the shoulders and hips with belts and straps. Later this garment was made in two parts, the front longer than the back. The longer front part, which could be curved, was gathered in deep folds to give an elegant shape.

The lower edges of Ethiopian clothes were trimmed with patterned braid and small tassels. This braid might be used along the front as well, to keep the gathered folds in place. A broad tasselled scarf or sash hanging over one shoulder and under the other arm, could also be worn.

The weapons of the Ethiopians included

# BIBLICAL DRESS

A loose linen garment like a shirt or shift was worn by the Hebrews and was common to both sexes. The chethomene, a tunic with a girdle around the waist, had straight sleeves, long or short, and was itself fairly straight, reaching the ankles. It also formed part of the ecclesiastical habit and was made of a fine linen. The tunics worn by labourers and servants were shorter with looser sleeves to permit freedom of movement. Wool and linen mixtures in the same garments were forbidden, being permitted for priests only, but garments of both kinds, unmixed, were worn, and winter tunics were probably made of fine wool.

Hebrew tunics had fringed borders with a ribbon or lace in blue and dark blue tassels called tsitsith. This decoration, which occurred also on cloaks, differentiated the Hebrews from other people. The girdle worn might be made of leather or richly embroidered, interthreaded with gold or decorated with precious stones. The richer the wearer, the more beautiful the decoration.

An over-tunic or robe was worn over the tunic and made in one piece with a lengthways slit running from the back to the chest. This was bound with ribbon. There were also slits at the sides for the arms to pass through; if sleeves were present they were added on, not an integral part of the garment.

A cloak or mantle (hyke) covered the whole body. It was made in different sizes and weights and could be up to 6 m long and 2 m wide (20 ft x 6 ft), serving as a complete item of clothing by day and a bed covering by night (as did the very similar plaid of the Scottish Highlanders). These mantles were worn by all classes and had fringes and blue ribboned edges.

The burnoose, another kind of hooded cloak, was worn by higher ranks. This could be made of skins and was usually ornamented with ermine and other furs. Another form of covering, rather like a smaller mantle or hyke, was a veil which was worn also to cover the face. In cold and wet weather a larger mantle similar to the hyke which covered the whole body was worn. A different type of mantle or veil which reached the feet was worn in warmer weather.

Thin gauze veils were in use among the Jewish ladies from the time of Solomon (c 973-933 BC). High ranking women wore tunics with coloured embroidery, linen girdles, sandals and cotton mantles.

A bride would wear a costume that included leg coverings, perhaps of brocade, reaching to the ankles.

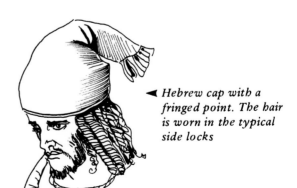

◄ *Hebrew cap with a fringed point. The hair is worn in the typical side locks*

The priest or rabbi on the left is in a highly decorated robe with fringing and an over-tunic. The man on the right is in a typical chethomene with long straight sleeves. The girdle, typical of the Biblical dress, was embroidered in a symmetrical design

## HEADWEAR

The turban, the usual headdress of the Persians, Arabs and Turks was also worn by Hebrew men. It varied in style and size according to rank. It was made with a small hemispherical scarlet cloth cap, the turban or long narrow band of linen, silk or muslin being folded round the bottom of the cap.

A diadem or gold fillet was worn on the turban by princes and the higher ranks. Diadems could be adorned with precious stones. Diadems and crowns were also worn by bridegrooms at their weddings.

Tiaras or bonnets were worn by Jews of both sexes and were ornamented. The bonnets of the priests were of linen and resembled truncated cones. Frontlets formed part of the Jewish headdress and consisted of scrolls of parchment inscribed with portions of the Law.

Turbans formed an essential part of ladies' headdress, and tiaras were also worn. Brides wore rows of gold or jewels around their headdresses and these descended down the cheeks and under the chin.

## HAIRSTYLES

Unlike the Egyptians, who shaved their heads, the Hebrews allowed their hair to grow quite long. To beautify it they sometimes powdered it with gold dust. Beards were also grown and trimmed with care.

Ladies' hair was braided, curled and plaited, and crispin pins or bodkins were used as hair ornamentation.

*The Jewish girl is in a loose linen shift-like dress with a narrow girdle. The headress has drum-shaped ear pieces*

## FOOTWEAR

Sandals were worn, which consisted of a sole with strings or bands attached to the upper surface to fasten it to the foot. Women's sandals were similar to those worn by the men except that they were more ornate, and they also wore leather slippers. They protected these when they were walking outside by wearing pattens to raise their feet above street level.

## JEWELLERY

Various kinds of bracelets for the arms, rings with or without a signet (signet rings being marks of authority) and gold neck chains with other decorative ornaments were all worn by the men of Israel. Chains and necklaces were popular with both men and women, and women also wore bracelets around their ankles. Earrings and diadems were worn by the women as well.

## MAKE-UP AND ACCESSORIES

The only cosmetic that ladies seem to have used was powder of lead ore for tinting their eyelids.

Women used ornamental mirrors and these were generally made of metal or brass. Perfume boxes that could be of gold encrusted with jewels were also worn around the neck and these were filled with musk or some other perfumed paste. A type of bag or purse was carried by most people to hold either food and necessities or money.

## MILITARY AND CLERGY

Protective clothing consisted of pectorals or breastplates, cloaks and a helmet. Large and smaller shields were carried by the soldiers, together with their weapons which were swords that could be two-edged, daggers, spears, javelins, bows and arrows and slings. The weapons were mainly made of bronze and iron. The pectoral, which could be made of linen, was covered with metal plates and attached to a short tunic. Belts made of brass or other metals were attached.

Priests wore a garment called the ephod on top of the chethomene. This was made of elaborately ornamented material, and was open-sided, sleeveless, and worn with a girdle.

*Soldier of Ancient Judaea*

19

# BABYLON AND ASSYRIA

Babylonian and Assyrian dress was simply cut. It generally consisted of a shift with short, tight sleeves similar to the Egyptian kalasiris; this was worn by both men and women, with or without a girdle. The higher ranking men wore their tunics longer, reading their feet, and when girdles were worn these were elaborately trimmed and embroidered.

## BABYLON

Babylonians wore two tunics. The under one was made of linen reaching to the feet, while the outer one was made of wool. Over these tunics a small white cloak (chlandion) was worn.

Babylonian men could wear a type of wrap-round kilt of woven material with a fringe along the edge. A fringed shawl could also be worn over the left shoulder, leaving the right arm free: the ends were tied together at the right hip.

Hair was generally black and short, being curly, but it could be worn longer, put up in a chignon at the back, and covered with a mitre cap or turban. Fillets were worn and

were often made of a thin strip of gold worn round the head across the brow. Another form of headwear was a round cap with a brim consisting of a broad band. Helmets worn in battle had pointed crowns.

Sandals were worn by both the Babylonians and the Assyrians and these differed from those of the Egyptians in having a leather piece at the back, covering the heels. Short boots were also worn. Soldiers wore knee-length leather boots, open up the front, with leather thong lacing.

Men wore signet rings and carried a staff or sceptre with an ornamented top.

Cosmetics were used, mainly black dye for the eyebrows and red for the lips. Perfumes and oils were also popular.

## ASSYRIA

For the Assyrians tunics and shawls were the chief garments. Their tunics were generally T-shaped and close fitting with elbow length sleeves and a round ornamented neckline. They reached either to the knees or down to the instep. Belts when worn were very wide with narrower belts over them. Shawls varied in size and could be draped in a variety of ways. Even the higher ranks wore these clothes, but their tunics generally reached to the feet. The girdles worn by the majority were trimmed with tassels and the tunics themselves elaborately embroidered and ornamented.

For ceremonial occasions a cloak-like overgarment was worn. This resembled a shoulder cape and was at first made of one piece of material worn under one arm and fastened with a clasp on the opposite shoulder. The cloak might also have a hole for the head to pass through, as well as one arm, with the other side open but hanging over both shoulders. Gradually these cloaks became more elaborate and were richly trimmed with fringes and tassels.

Women's tunics were generally long with

*Assyrian headdress* ▶

◀ *Babylonian Royal headdress*

*Assyrian truncated hat* ▶

◀ *Assyrian hairstyle with ornamentation*

three-quarter length sleeves and the belts, if worn, were narrow.

## HAIRSTYLES AND HEADWEAR

The Assyrians had bushy black hair which was allowed to grow long. Wigs could also be worn. Thick beards and moustaches were popular and very often they too were artificial.

A fillet or band was usually worn around the head and women, if a head covering was required, drew their shawls over the head. Men could wear a tall-crowned felt cap which tapered slightly towards the top. Hanging tassels from the top might fall to waist level.

## JEWELLERY AND ACCESSORIES

Gold bracelets, armbands and earrings were all popular. 'Dog collar' necklaces were also often worn. Fans and parasols were carried by the slaves for their mistresses.

## MILITARY

The Assyrian soldiers in the time of Xerxes (c 519-465 BC) wore brass helmets and carried short swords, bucklers and javelins similar to those of the Egyptians. The pectorals worn were of linen.

The Assyrian infantry wore long tunics, similar to those of civilians, with both broad and narrow belts. The helmets were tall and conical. Elliptical-shaped shields, some large enough to protect the whole body, were carried.

The cavalry wore wrap-around kilts over which were worn waist-length chain mail corselets. Boots reached up almost to the knees and mail was worn over the knees to protect them. The cavalry were armed with swords, bows and arrows, javelins, spears, slings, etc.

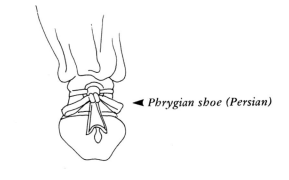

◄ *Phrygian shoe (Persian)*

Only priests wore bleached linen and this was made up into a long, short-sleeved tunic with an upper garment that was wound around the body. A one-piece cloak drawn under one arm and fastened on the opposite shoulder was also worn. An apron was sometimes adopted, one style reaching from the waist to the knees and edged with braid and tassels. The apron was kept in place with cords that had tasselled ends.

_____ CEREMONIAL _____

Higher Court and State officials wore a long fringed stole or shoulder scarf, the ends being wound around the body. The richness of the fringing on this scarf indicated high rank, even more than the amount of trimming and decoration on the tunic or skirt.

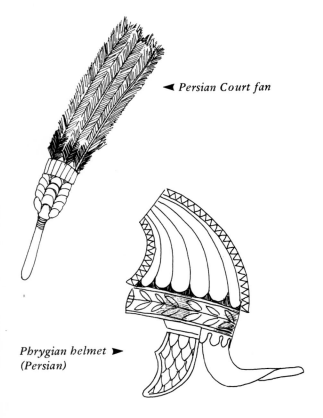

◄ *Persian Court fan*

*Phrygian helmet ►*
*(Persian)*

# PERSIA AND MEDIA

## PERSIAN

The Persians took their dress from the Medes. It consisted of tiaras, cidaris, and mitres (all head coverings), tunics with sleeves and anaxyrides (a type of loose baggy trousers) to which was added the candys or mantle. The hose and breeches which they wore with blouse-like sleeved shirts differed greatly from the dress of other nations of the period.

Originally the Persians wore tanned leather, covering the whole body including the legs, and their clothing had therefore to be adapted to the size of the skins. The coat was thus made of two or three pieces with the sleeves cut separately and then sewn in. It was knee length, open down the front and had fairly tight-fitting long sleeves.

The leg coverings were wide and reached down to the knees or ankles.

The dress of the women was very similar to that of the men except that their coats were often longer and wider and closed down the front, with just a slit open at the breast. High-ranking Persian women wore robes that trailed on the ground and were almost always of linen, wool not being popular amongst the ladies.

## FOOTWEAR

The footwear of both the Medes and the Persians was very primitive, comprising simply of pieces of leather or some other strong material tied to the feet over the instep.

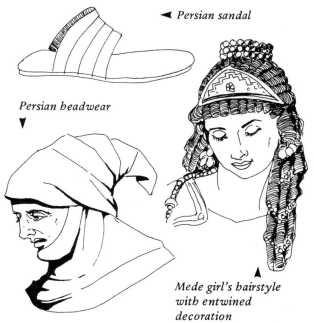

◄ *Persian sandal*

*Persian headwear*
▼

▲
*Mede girl's hairstyle with entwined decoration*

## HEADWEAR AND HAIRSTYLES

The headdress of the Persians consisted of a cap or mitre, coming down in front to cover the forehead to the eyebrows and at the back to the nape of the neck. The cap also had flaps at the sides covering the ears and these were sometimes long enough to be tied under the chin. The cap was generally made of a stiffish material such as leather or felt. Another style of headdress, a high, domed cap with lappets which could be tied in the front was called a Phrygian cap. The tip of this style came to a point.

Hair was generally thick and curly and was worn shorter than that of the Assyrians. Moustaches were almost always worn but beards were not so usual.

Persian soldiers wore trousers and tunics covered with iron plates like the scales of a fish. A leather belt around the waist had a sheath to contain either a dagger or sword. This was also fastened to the hips or thighs.

Breastplates and shields were worn as well as helmets which were sometimes ornamented with plumes of horse-hair. The horses were protected by plated coats of armour and forehead and thigh pieces.

The famous Persian Archers were usually dressed in the Median style of long tunics with close-fitting sleeves worn over trousers. Coloured sashes were worn around the waist. The headwear was high and bowl shaped with earflaps. The Grand Guard of the Persians, the Immortals, so called because as fast as one of them was killed his place was taken by another, wore tunics that were often embroidered with gold and pearls.

# MEDE

The dress of the Medes was made of finer materials than Persian costume and the gowns were longer and more voluminous with wide sleeves. The candys worn by the men was fuller at the base and so long that it had to be gathered up at the front and sides and held by a girdle. Its long sleeves were wide at the wrists, becoming tight-fitting towards the top of the arms.

The Medes seldom wore breeches or hose but when they did, they resembled those of the Persians.

## HEADWEAR

The headdress of the ordinary Median people was a type of hood surrounding the face and concealing the chin as well as covering the head. It had two broad ribbons attached, one hanging over the front and the other allowed to hang behind.

*Persian Immortal Archer' in long-skirted loose-fitting tunic with wide, flowing sleeves. Hair and beard are plaited*

The upper classes wore a different kind of cap which varied in height, the crown usually

## ROMAN

The young man is wearing a plain woollen material toga candida over a short sleeved under garment. The woman is in a long under garment or tunica interior over which was worn a draped stola. Her hair is in the fashionable built up style, frizzed and curled.

The soldier is in a lorica of overlapping metal scales worn over a rust coloured tunic and close fitting breeches. His helmet is of iron and he carries a rectangular shield and also weapons.

## DRESS OF THE CELTIC PEOPLE

The man on the left is wearing a knee length tunic over which is worn a large cloak or mantle with an aperture in the centre for the head to pass through. This was made of a yarn woven in a check pattern.

The woman is in a close fitting high-necked chemise over which is worn a long sleeveless tunic and a cloak fastened on one shoulder with a fibula.

The man in the background is a Roman official wearing a toga praetexta.

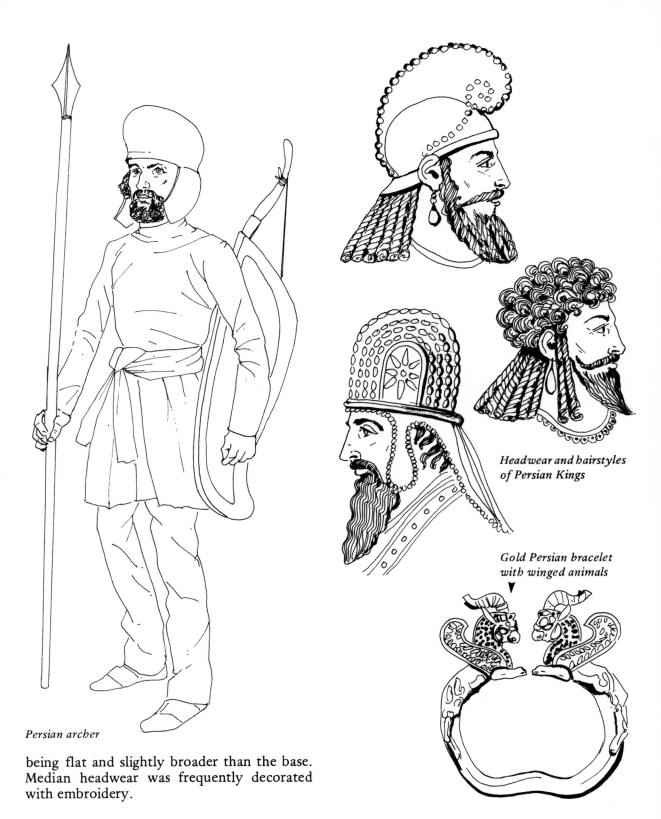

*Persian archer*

*Headwear and hairstyles of Persian Kings*

*Gold Persian bracelet with winged animals*

being flat and slightly broader than the base. Median headwear was frequently decorated with embroidery.

*Greek poet Anacreon dancing with Bacchus and Cupid*

# GREECE

We know a great deal about the clothes worn by the Greeks, from surviving statues and from the many thousands of painted vases now in museums. The most striking thing about Greek costume is that it was entirely draped, consisting of lengths of material of varying sizes and shapes held together with pins or fibulae, and fastened with one or more girdles. Throughout the period (from the seventh to the first centuries BC) men and women wore very similar clothes: a Greek wife could and probably often did wear her husband's cloak out of doors.

## TUNICS

The basic garment of both sexes was the tunic, worn ankle length by women, and only to the knees by men, except on ceremonial occasions. The tunic (for which the Greek word is chiton) was originally made of two rectangular pieces of material joined together at the shoulders by pins and with a cord or belt at the waist. Men often wore two belts, one at the waist and one around the hips. Later, a type of sleeved chiton was introduced. This was made by using larger rectangles of material, which thus hung over the arms as far as the elbow. They were pinned together at intervals with fibulae.

Two peoples exerted an important influence over Greek fashions. The Dorians, from Illyria, invaded Greece in about 1100 BC, and introduced the simple woollen tunic. When worn by women this was long and often called a peplos. In the sixth century BC the Greeks came into contact with the Ionians of Asia Minor, and finer, linen garments became fashionable. There were thus two types of tunic, the Doric and the Ionic. The Doric chiton was always sleeveless and made of wool, the Ionic chiton generally of linen, so that the drapes were more elegant, and could even be pleated, the pleats being starched in. It was made so long that the extra material was pulled through the waistband, giving a bloused effect. The sleeves could be pinned or sewn on, and could be quite ample. The top of the Ionic chiton was loose fitting and was kept in place with either shoulder straps or cross bands. Two girdles were sometimes worn, one around the waist and another higher up. When the buildings on the Acropolis were excavated, a large number of statues were found of young girls dressed either in the Doric peplos or the Ionic chiton.

In later years, it became fashionable for women to wear the ground length chiton with the peplos on top. The peplos could either hang loose to just below the waist or it could be long and fastened with a girdle. A further alternative was to use a very long piece of material in front, and to make a fold at the shoulders, so that an extra flap of material fell to waist level. This fold was known as a diploidion.

In Sparta, girls wore short tunics, slit at the sides, revealing the thighs, as they were expected to take part in the same sports and physical exercises as the boys.

Tunics were made in a variety of colours, usually light, and often had ornamented borders of flowers or geometrical designs.

The belt or girdle worn with a tunic could be made in a variety of materials, according

*Greek girl holding a laurel headdress and wearing a Doric tunic*

to the rank of the wearer. High ranking Greeks in particular went in for much colour and embroidery in their girdles. The zona was a broad girdle worn by women, which could be fringed.

Working men and slaves wore a special type of tunic called the exomis. This was shorter than the normal tunic and was only fastened over the left shoulder, leaving the right arm unencumbered.

## CLOAKS AND MANTLES

Grecian mantles were sometimes white but could also be in dark colours, including purple. Both the colour and material depended on the rank and circumstances of the wearer. The himation was worn over a tunic and could be single or double if it was cold. This was made of a large, almost square, piece of material, and was worn draped over the shoulders like a shawl, or as a cloak and head covering. It might also be made of a delicate transparent material, silk becoming fashionable after its introduction from India in the fourth century BC. It fastened on the right shoulder with a fibula or buckle and reached to about the knee, the right arm being left free.

Men also wore the chlamys, a kind of short cloak fastened on one shoulder, over a short chiton or on its own.

The tribon or tribonion (the philosopher's mantle) was similar to the ordinary himation except that it was generally brown or black and was usually threadbare, dirty and patched. It was worn thus to demonstrate poverty and a contempt for earthly vanities. In Athens it was worn also by advocates at the bar.

The chlaena or laena was a Greek garment of military origin that acted as a surtout in bad weather and as a bed covering as well. It was a square shape and could be lined. The chlanis or chlanidon was similar to the laena but in a softer and lighter weight material. This could be worn by women as well as men. The sisyra was another mantle rather

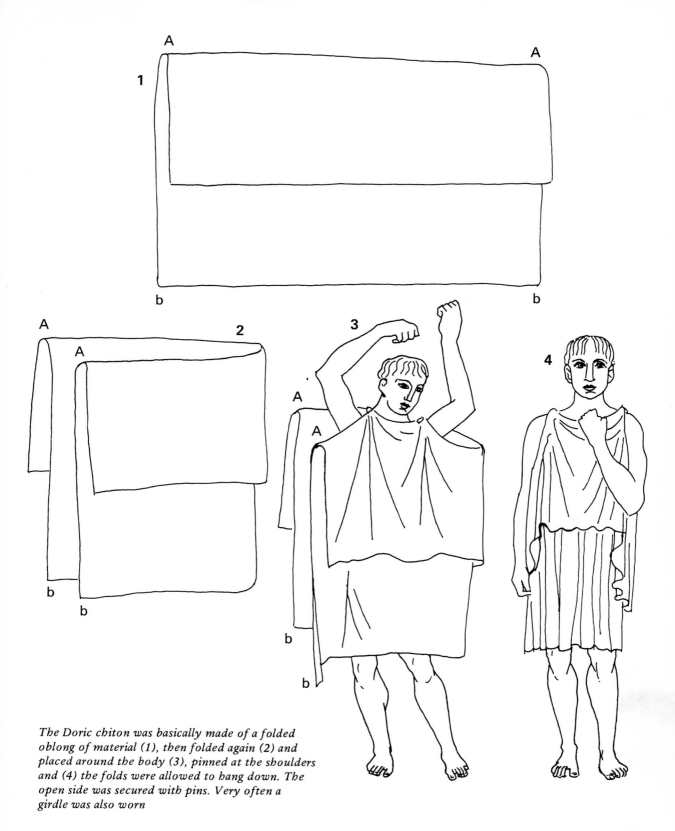

The Doric chiton was basically made of a folded oblong of material (1), then folded again (2) and placed around the body (3), pinned at the shoulders and (4) the folds were allowed to hang down. The open side was secured with pins. Very often a girdle was also worn

The lady on the left is in a Doric peplos fastened by fibulae over the Ionic dress. The lady on the right is in an Ionic chiton fastened along the shoulders and down the arms with clasps

*The young Greek lady with the elaborately raised hairstyle is wearing a Doric chiton with a clasp over the long Ionic tunic. The lady on the right has a peplos over her gown which has a girdle around the waist*

31

Greek peasants

The Greek man is in a simple travelling dress with his petasos (hat) slung over his shoulders. On his feet are sandals that are held on with thonging between the toes. The Greek lady on the right is wearing a short-sleeved peplos over a chiton and has a simple hairstyle gathered in a knot on top of her head

33

like the laena; this, again, was in a thick material and could be used as a bed covering.

The tarentine worn by Greek women and very occasionally also by men was white and of such thin material that the form of the body was visible through it. A veil or light summer cloak was also worn by women and known as the theristrion. This did not cover the head and, if required, a hat or tholia was worn. Also worn by women was an outer garment called a crocotula (its name was derived from the word crocus because of its saffron colour).

## HAIRSTYLES

Before the Persian Wars (*c* 480 BC), men wore their hair long, in elaborately curled tresses and fastened with gold pins. Later however, young Athenian men cut their hair on coming of age and consecrated it to the Gods. A few of the elegant upper classes kept their hair long, but most wore it close-cropped, as we can see from numerous statues and reliefs. Until the fifth century BC beards were usual, but later they were seen only on older men.

Greek women usually wore their hair long, in braids drawn into a knot behind, and with a central parting. They also made use of a kind of scarf called a kekryphalos, which gathered the hair from the nape of the neck and the forehead and piled it on top of the head. Hair was often tinted, blonde being the most popular colour, and artificial locks and wigs were also worn. Combs were made of olive wood, bone, ivory, shell, bronze, and were often elaborately carved.

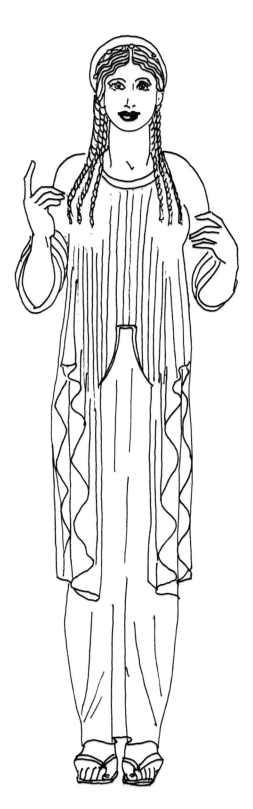

◄ *The man on the left is in an Ionic chiton, bloused, with a girdle around the waist to adjust the length. The lady is in a long chiton with the himation over one shoulder. The man on the right is in a long Doric chiton fastened on the left arm with a pin*

*The Greek lady is wearing an Ionic chiton and open* ► *sandals*

*The goddess Ceres in a peplos with a girdle*

*Hairstyle of Athenian* ▶
*youth*

*Greek headdresses*

37

Hats were seldom worn by the Greeks except in extremes of weather, although soldiers did wear helmets and some form of headwear was worn on ceremonial occasions or when travelling.

The kyne was a leather bonnet worn mostly by slaves and the lower classes. More elegant was the pilos, a pointed conical hat with a narrow brim and somtimes a peak to protect the eyes from the sun. It was usually made of felt, but could be of leather or even metal. It was sometimes worn inside a helmet as a lining.

For travelling the petasos, a wide-brimmed low-crowned hat of felt or straw was worn. It was fastened under the chin by a lace, and could thus be worn hung over the back.

Women might cover their heads with a fold of their gowns, or else wear the tholia, a wide-brimmed round hat with a pointed centre.

_____ FOOT AND LEGWEAR _____

The Greeks usually went barefoot, shoes and sandals being worn only as protection or on special occasions. The shoes worn by both Greeks and Romans can be divided into two groups. One type covered the whole foot and sometimes reached to the mid-calf and the other covered only the sole of the foot and was fastened with leather thonging.

*The Greek soldier is wearing a travelling cloak fastened at the front with an ornamental brooch, and a hat or petasos*

Sandals consisted of a sole of cork, wood or leather, kept on the foot by laces tied around the ankle and toes. The embas was a shoe of the second type, with laces up the front and the top turned down. The endromis was a similar type of boot, but without a turned down top. These last two types of footwear were worn by travellers.

Another type of shoe worn by Athenian priests and also by the Romans was usually made of a thin, light, white leather which covered the whole foot.

Buskins or cothurnoi, which originated in Greece were made to fit either foot and had elevated soles which added to the height of the wearer. A binding was fastened to the sole and this was passed between the big toe and the second toe, divided into two and passed through the latchet, securing the sole

*Greek footwear*

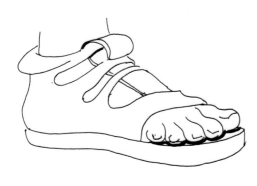

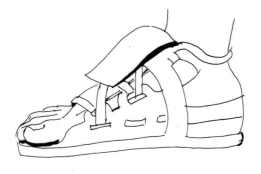

to the feet. The two bands were criss-crossed high up the legs and then fastened. Buskins were worn by both men and women.

Greek women, who spent most of their time in the house, wore only a type of sole attached with straps, similar to sandals, when they did go out. Later, from about the fourth century BC more elegant shoes were worn, red with yellow edged soles being very popular. There were many forms of shoes, ranging from simple sandals to boots that laced high and could have slits and a variety of decorations.

Breeches (anaxyrides) were well known to the ancient Greeks, but were regarded as a barbarian garment and not adopted by them. Pythagoras (the Greek philosopher c 582-500 BC) is said to have worn them, but they never became fashionable.

The Greeks did not generally wear any leg coverings beneath the tunic, except when at war, when they wore greaves and military boots. The knemis of the Greeks (called by the Romans ocrea) was a greave or form of leg armour made of metal such as bronze, copper or iron. It covered the front and sides of the leg and reached no further than the instep so as not to impede free movement. The greave was fastened at the back with clasps or fibulae.

Greaves of leather were also worn by country labourers and were a kind of boot leg. They were made of thick or double leather, reaching above the knees and descending to the instep, fastened at the back with straps and buckles. Both for fighting and country wear greaves were often worn on the lower leg only. Some had ornamented or indented borders at the top.

———————JEWELLERY———————

Elaborate items of gold jewellery and ornaments in the hair were worn by Athenian men before the Persian Wars. Later, however, a ring would be the only usual form of male jewellery, and this would have a carved stone set into it for impressing seals. It seems, however, that some of the young and wealthy dandies in Athens also wore anklets and probably other items of jewellery as well.

Earrings were fashionable and were sometimes worn by high-ranking young men as well as by women, children and servants. The ears were pierced and the earrings made of the most precious metals available, and sometimes decorated with rose shapes.

Necklaces were worn, and were often of gold. In the Mycenaean period, pendants and necklaces were elaborate and heavy, but these were replaced in the Classical period by lighter necklets, from which amulets might hang to ward off the 'evil eye'.

Bracelets were popular among the Greeks, and could be worn on the upper arm between the elbow and the shoulder as well as on the wrist. Often they consisted of a simple band of gold and silver, but they could be spiral shaped, or in the form of a coiling snake, and ornamented with precious stones. It was fashionable to wear bangles around the ankle or calf, and these periscelides could be decorated with tinkling bells. Wealthy women would keep their jewellery in coffers and would have slaves to help them adorn themselves.

## MAKE-UP AND ACCESSORIES

Greek women made use of beauty creams, rouge and perfumes. Athens had its own perfume market, where perfumes were sold in specially shaped vases. Ladies of high rank might use ceruse, which was a whitish colour, to give themselves clear-looking complexions, and pink alkanet to make their cheeks rosy, but it was not regarded as genteel to be over made-up. Courtesans, on the other hand, often enlarged their eyes with black and brown lines.

To eradicate unwanted hair women used plasters, razors, or pulled the hairs out with small tweezers.

Many articles of Greek ladies' toilet have been found, including hairpins, curling tongs, razors, scissors and nail files. Mirrors were usually of polished metal, for although the existence of glass was known, it was seldom used.

## MILITARY

Helmets were worn by the Greeks and the Romans in times of war and there were several kinds in use by the Greeks from as early as the time of Homer. The ancient Grecian helmets were generally made of bronze and frequently ornamented with gold and silver.

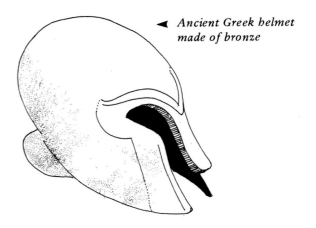
◄ *Ancient Greek helmet made of bronze*

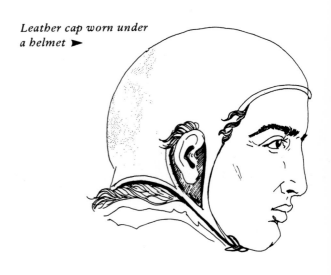
*Leather cap worn under a helmet* ►

The Greek kyne was a helmet with a type of elevated ridge going from the back over to the front and curving forward, which was ornamental as well as a defence for the head. This crest was often decorated with real or imitation horse-hair or, after the time of Homer, feather plumes. The helmets belonging to the chief commanders in the Grecian and Trojan armies were distinguished by having three or even four such crests with a horse-hair crest over them all. Helmets in this period were fastened beneath the chin with a strap or leather thong which could be decorated with embroidery.

A cap made of leather resembling a helmet but without a crest, called a kataityx, was generally worn by young men approaching manhood and also as protection for the head.

Another type of leather helmet in the Homeric period was strengthened on the inside with interwoven thongs, ornamented on the outside with bear's teeth, and often lined with a pileus or woollen cap. Many Greek helmets had some form of protection for the face, such as a nose-guard or a kind of grating or metal network which covered the face entirely.

The body armour used by the Ancient Greeks consisted of a short leather tunic with a left sleeve only, the right sleeve being that of an under tunic of softer and more flexible material. The tunic was open at the sides below the girdle.

The Greeks also employed the thorax for military wear. This was a large breastplate, perhaps of brass and often highly ornamented, fixed to a short and sleeveless tunic which could be of leather or other material, to which metal shoulder-guards were also

*The Greek soldier is a hoplite. He is wearing a corselet* ►
*of leather covered in overlapping metal plates. The*
*two shoulder pieces are secured at the back and laced*
*in the front. From the waist down are strips of*
*leather worn over a very short chiton. The helmet*
*is of the Doric style with a large ornamental horse-*
*hair crest*

connected. The shoulder-guards were then
fastened to the thorax at the front with
thongs or cords which could be unfastened
easily when necessary. The thorax was large
enough to cover the whole front as far down
as the navel and extended round to the back.
It could also have an extension made up of
broad straps, that could be of leather and
metal plated, which reached down almost to
the base of the under tunic, or be worn with a
zona or girdle of metal beneath it. The
thorax was not always made of metal but,
like the pectoral, might be of linen and was
not only lighter in weight but also deflected
the points of the enemies' weapons effectively.
Alexander the Great, who had obtained a
shirt of this type at the Battle of Issus (333
BC) wore them in preference thereafter.
The thorax underwent a variety of changes
during the period it was in use until it formed
a complete body armour covering both back
and front.

Greek shields varied in both form and
size. They might be round, square or rectangular, and decorated with circular designs
or engravings.

Sword blades were generally of iron and
the hilts decorated with gold or silver studs;
the scabbards were also richly embellished.
The sword-belt or baldrick, worn over the
right shoulder across the front and back to
the left hip where it was fastened with a
buckle, was attached to the scabbard of the
sword and was also often highly ornamented.

*Front and back of
Greek breast cuirass*

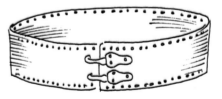

*Bronze belt*

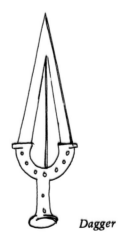

*Dagger*

# ROME

## TUNICS AND TOGAS

An early Roman costume consisted of a type of shirt or tunica made of white woollen cloth and worn with a cloak. The tunica usually came to just below the knees, although soldiers wore it shorter and bridegrooms generally wore it down to the ground. Some tunics had elbow length sleeves but later, when two tunics could be worn at once, one could have long sleeves. In winter as many as four woollen tunics might be worn at once.

The Senators of Rome had a distinguishing broad purple stripe known as a latus clavus sewn on to the front of their tunics. The Knights, who were not so eminent had two narrower stripes of the same colour, and this was known as an angustus clavus.

Romans did not always wear girdles indoors but were never seen without them outdoors. The girdles also acted as purses where money and other valuables could be kept. From about the third century AD the dalmatica whose distinctive feature was its

*Demosthenes wearing a Greek garment which was* ▶
*the fore-runner of the Roman toga*

43

wide sleeves replaced the tunica. Basically a tunic, it had a rounded neckline and was calf or ankle length and decorated with coloured bands. Originally worn without a belt, it later had a belt added and this was worn over the hips.

The earliest Roman costume consisted of nothing but the toga, which was basically one semi-circular piece of material (sometimes, two pieces joined together) which was worn draped round the body in one of several ways to make a long loose gown which might be open but was more popularly open only at the top down to the waist. The toga was folded in many different ways through the centuries but a typical mode would be as follows. It was worn without sleeves, the right arm being left free while the left shoulder was covered, and the material, with an opening to enable the arm to pass through, allowed to hang down in folds to the ground either side of the arm. The toga was not belted around the waist like the tunic, but part of the material was twisted around the body, thrown over the left shoulder, passed across the back, brought forward under the right arm and again thrown over the left shoulder, the resulting protuberance being allowed to fall in folds which could be used as a pocket. The part of the toga that passed over the left shoulder could be drawn over the head as protection from the sun or bad weather, or on ceremonial occasions.

The size and shape of the toga varied as did the materials it was made of. The toga was at first (from the sixth century BC) no longer than the chlamys, but it became longer as time passed. The early Romans wore a toga which was straight and close fitting, just covering the arms and reaching down to the feet. By the time of the Emperors however (c first to second century AD) the toga measured more than 7 m (23 ft) across and as it became more voluminous and its folds increased, the material was draped

◄ *Toga worn draped over the head*

44

carefully, not only for elegance but also for convenience and to prevent it from getting dirty. The toga was originally made of white woollen cloth but as time went on more expensive materials were used, even silk. Colours and embroidery were also introduced.

The usual toga was the toga virilis or pura which was made of plain unbleached wool. The toga praetexta, with a broad purple border was worn by officials, by young men up to the age of seventeen, by young women until they married and by priests and judges. Once a young man had reached seventeen he wore the man's toga, the toga virilis, but it was usual for him to keep one arm within its folds for the first year.

The toga candida (white toga) was worn by candidates for public office and was like the toga virilis except that it was of bleached wool. The toga picta and the tunica palmata were triumphal garments. They both had a purple background with gold embroidery. The toga pulla, in dark sombre colours, was worn for mourning.

The toga was rarely worn at home, a tunic more often being preferred. A tunic might also be worn beneath the toga, reaching usually to the knees only, or on its own by ordinary Roman citizens who could not afford a toga. The toga was not worn for festivals either, a special garment, the synthesis, being worn. Although this had a Greek name the synthesis was of Roman origin and was a loose dress of the mantle or pallium type which was easy to put on and take off.

The trabea was a gown worn to show honour and distinction. Similar to the toga and resembling the chlamys or mantle, the trabea was made in a superior quality material and had stripes across the chest. It was generally also slightly shorter than a toga.

For women there were several kinds of tunics which went under various different names. The tunica regilla or tunica recta for example was a kind of white tunic worn by Roman virgins before marriage. Sometimes more than one tunic was worn at a time in which case the one next to the skin was called a subucula while the outer one was called the tunica exterior. Tunics were worn until the third century AD. They later became known as caracallae.

The basic garment, the stola, was worn by women throughout the period and was similar to the Ionic chiton. The stola was made fuller than the tunica with the sleeves forming part of the fullness, and fell to the ground. It was belted at the hips and under the bust and was fastened at the shoulders with fibulae. Beneath this garment women wore a simple, sleeveless tunica.

The dalmatica worn by women was longer than that of the men, sometimes trailing to the ground. From the fourth century the dalmatica was wider at the hem and its sleeves less square. A belt was worn around the waist or slightly higher. The dalmatica was worn over a calf length tunic with long sleeves, narrower towards the wrists. The tunic was decorated with embroidery and coloured bands. The ensemble, with a veil, formed the foundation of women's dress until the end of the thirteenth century AD.

All Roman women wore girdles which, when worn out of doors, often had a purse attached to carry valuables. A broad band, or strophium, around their breasts acted as a bodice and was buckled on the left shoulder.

## CLOAKS AND MANTLES

In bad weather a bell-shaped cloak known as a paenula could be worn. The paenula was usually worn closed all round but could be left open down the front. When closed the sides were lifted to allow more freedom for the arms. It was made in various lengths: sometimes the sides were shorter than the front and back, and sometimes the back was pointed, sometimes rounded. The paenula usually had an attached hood. It could be worn by both sexes, although its wear by women was not always approved of: the Emperor Alexander Severus (AD 208-235) forbade the matrons of Rome to wear it

46

within the city although they were permitted to wear it in the country.

The byrrus was another form of cloak, which was usually red in colour. It had a cowl and gradually cowls or head coverings became known by that name.

The pallium, like the Greek himation and worn in similar fashion, was the usual attire of philosophers and learned men. From the fourth century AD it was folded more and more until it was so narrow that it resembled a stole.

The Roman lacerna, a large cloak or mantle worn over other clothing in inclement weather, had an open front fastened with fibulae or buckles and a cowl or hood attached in such a way that it could be removed easily. For winter wear the lacerna was made of a thick, warm material (it might even be of fur) while for summer the materials were softer and lighter. Generally the lacerna was in black or dark brown but the Senators or people of higher rank wore purple or scarlet for distinction. The lacerna was originally a military garment but when the toga began to be worn less frequently, in the second century AD, it was more universally adopted and was generally worn by those who frequented the public shows. It was always set aside as a mark of respect when the Emperor entered the theatre.

The sagum or paludamentum was a military mantle derived from the Gauls which was worn by the Romans. It was a large, open cloak made of woollen material with clasp fastenings. When worn by generals or high ranking officers it was scarlet with a purple border. Originally it had sleeves but these were not seen in the Roman versions. The paludamentum became more popular with the rise of the Byzantine Empire (fourth century AD).

The palliolum, a short mantle or cowl or hood, was worn to cover the head. It was worn by the sick (and also by Roman women of ill fame not wishing to be recognised).

The caracalla was also a kind of pallium or mantle and was Gallic in origin. It was introduced to the Romans by the Emperor Antoninus (AD 188-217) who was given the nickname of Caracalla. The caracalla was a large, loose garment with sleeves (in this differing from the lacerna which was sleeveless) and a hood. Originally it reached only to the middle of the thighs, but the Emperor always wore it down to his feet.

The palla, the outer garment worn by Roman women, was similar to the Greek peplos, and the ladies sometimes covered their heads as well as their arms with it. It was made of a rectangular piece of woven wool and, like the toga, was at first not very large but became more voluminous towards the end of the Republican era. At first the palla was worn in similar fashion to the toga but later it enclosed the entire body and arms and was secured with a fibula on the left shoulder.

Roman ladies could also wear a robe or mantle which was known as cyclas because of its rotund form.

Roman slaves wore clothing similar to that of the poor. Their dress was always in a dark colour and consisted of a sleeveless tunic, or the lacerna with a hood. On their feet they wore crepidae, a type of sandal.

## HAIRSTYLES

In very early times, Roman men wore their hair long, but later short styles became popular, with the hair brushed forward from the crown. In Imperial Rome curled and waved hair, longer and sometimes dyed, became fashionable. The perfuming of hair was quite common, even in the army. In the fourth century AD a circular cut with the hair turned under all round was a fashionable

*The Roman lady's costume is made of a lighter and softer material than a man's. The man on the right is wearing a short tunic, popular until about the thirteenth century AD. He is wearing high buskins*

Byzantine style.

Baldness was considered a deformity and Julius Caesar (100-44 BC) wore a laurel crown to conceal his lack of hair. Perukes or false hair were not known at that time, though they were later worn by Emperors who had need of such devices.

In times of mourning the Greeks cut their hair and shaved their beards but the Romans allowed both to grow and left their hair untidy, sometimes covering it with dust and ashes. (Ornamentation was not worn at such a time and a black garment resembling the lacerna was adopted.)

In early Rome beards were usual but later they were seen only on older men. Publius Ticinius Maenas brought barbers from Sicily and introduced the fashion for shaving which held good until the time of Hadrian (AD 76-138), who in fact revived the practice of wearing beards in his lifetime only. Young Roman men started shaving their beards from the time they assumed the toga virilis or, more usually, from the age of twenty one. It was usual to celebrate the first shaving by holding a festival where gifts were offered. The beard was not always entirely shaven off, but sometimes just clipped.

In wealthy families slaves, often female, were sometimes kept for the purpose of dressing the hair and for shaving. For the poorer classes barbers' shops were available.

Professors of philosophy let their hair and

Roman headwear and headdress

Roman general's hairstyle with laurel leaves

48

EGYPTIAN, ASSYRIAN, HEBREW

*The woman is wearing a simple figure-revealing dress of linen in the Egyptian fashion. The man, also Egyptian is wearing a schenti (loincloth) secured around the waist. He is wearing a painted headcloth.*

*The centre figure is an Assyrian woman with an ankle length tunic and jewelled collar high around the neck. Over the tunic is seen the long rectangular shawl, fringed at the edge.*

*The Hebrew Levite (under-priest) is in a long, ankle length, white woollen tunic with close fitting sleeves. Over the tunic is wound a narrow ribbon decorated with silver ornaments. The conical hat is of felt with a twisted band of linen around the base.*

## GREEK AND PERSIAN

*The man on the left is wearing a short chlamys or travelling cloak which is fastened by a brooch on one shoulder. This is usually worn over a short chiton. The woman is wearing a Doric chiton, the early Greek style rectangular shaped garment, over which was worn the peplos.*

*The Persian Immortal spearman is in the Persian style long, loose fitting tunic with wide sleeves, decorated with geometric motifs.*

beards grow long in order to make themselves look wise. Slaves also wore long hair and beards, in this case for distinguishing purposes, but when they were given their freedom their hair and beards were shaven off and they wore a woollen cap known as a pileus. Survivors of shipwrecks as well as those acquitted of crimes also shaved their hair.

During the period of the Roman Republic the hairstyles of the women were fairly simple and consisted of just a row of curls across the front with a knot at the nape of the neck. The hair had a centre parting and was slightly waved. Another style, in Greek fashion, had a chignon on the top of the head.

This simplicity in hairstyles was lost as the Romans became wealthy and powerful although the less well-off continued to wear simple styles with a parting and the hair gathered in a knot. For the wealthy, curls, locks, plaits and waves were arranged in the most complicated fashion and hot irons were used both to frizz and curl the hair which was sometimes raised very high by rows of curls one upon the other into the form of a helmet. It could also be worn in a cluster of curls at the front with a high chignon. If the ladies did not have sufficient hair of their own, false hair was added to complete the required height.

Blonde hair was so admired by the Romans that they often bleached their own as well as oiling and perfuming it. Hair powders were not in use at this time.

Women of rank had slaves to arrange their hair, while they themselves just held the mirror and gave directions. Married women were distinguishable from single girls by the way they divided their hair into two parts.

The hair was not only arranged in a great variety of elaborate styles but was adorned with gold, pearls and other precious stones and also occasionally with garlands or chaplets of flowers. Hair was also bound with various coloured ribbons, or with broad bands embellished with embroidery and encrusted with precious stones. A net or hair caul sometimes enclosed the back hair and was in general

*Matron or widow's elaborate headdress in the Roman period*

*Greek style hair fashion in the Roman period*

*Himation drawn over the head, Greek style*

*Second century Flavian period hairstyle*

use among Roman women. These nets were generally enriched with embroidery or gold thread. Hairpins and combs of gold or ivory were much in evidence, as were kerchiefs and fillets.

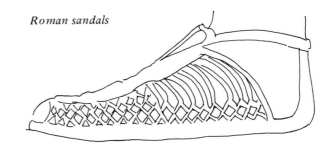

*Roman sandals*

## HEADWEAR

The Romans often covered their head with part of the toga which they removed when meeting superiors. Mantles such as the paenula, lacerna and byrrus with their attached hoods were also worn and these hoods could be thrown back on to the shoulders at any time.

The galerus, a type of cap resembling a helmet, was worn by the Romans as was the infula, a white woollen band tied around the head and fastened with a knot behind so that the two ends hung down on each side. This was mainly worn as a ceremonial ornament. The pileus, or woollen cap, was also worn by the Romans at public games and festivals, by slaves who had obtained their freedom and by the aged and infirm for warmth.

The headdress of the early Roman women was quite simple. They seldom went out in public and when they did they always covered their head with a veil. More ornaments were, however, worn as the Romans became wealthier. Veils were fashionable from the start of the Byzantine era.

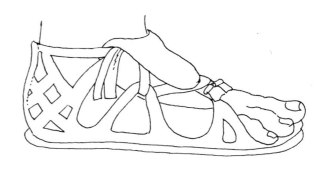

## FOOT AND LEGWEAR

The Romans, who often travelled far afield to cold climates, attached more importance to their footwear than the Greeks. In addition to sandals (known in Latin by such names as crepida and sandalium) they wore shoes that covered the whole foot (calceus) and heavy military boots (caliga). The men of ancient Latium wore shoes made of untanned leather called perones. It was not until much later that tanned leather was used and this was made in various colours, untanned leather being left in the main to the lower

*Roman buskin* ▶

*Roman calcei*

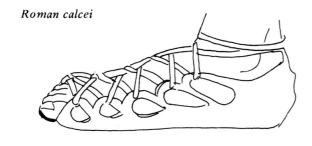

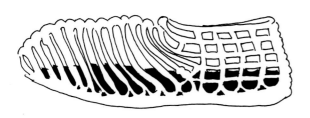

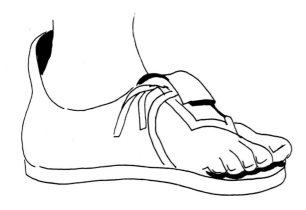

classes and to countrymen. Wooden-soled shoes were also worn by country people and the poor.

The bindings of the crepida, or sandal, sometimes reached to the calf. Another style of sandal, the baxea, was made of the leaves of a palm tree. The solea was a sandal often worn in the country with a tunic and mantle or for travelling. These sandals could also be worn at feasts but they were always removed when eating.

The calceus covered the foot and was fastened with lacing or thongs. It often had high soles of cork or some other light material to give extra height to the wearer and was worn with the toga or for travelling.

The caliga was a military shoe or sandal made up of a thick sole fastened with strong bindings or thongs which reached above the ankles. These shoes were sometimes strengthened with nails and were chiefly worn by the ordinary soldiers. Another style, the campagus, was worn by Emperors and army generals. It did not differ much from the caliga but the bindings were more closely interwoven and crossed over more, giving a network effect.

The Romans distinguished the shoes of high ranking people by their colours and form. For instance, no-one who had not served in the office of aedile (magistrate) could wear the shoes known as mullaei which were red. These shoes were first worn by the ancient kings of Alba and then by the kings of Rome, only after the expulsion of King Tarquin being worn by the chief magistrates. However black shoes were worn by Senators and people of rank and the ordinary people prior to the end of the Republic. Senators wore high shoes fastened with thonging decorated with gold or silver crescent ornaments which were peculiar to them.

The shoes of the wealthier classes in general were painted in various colours and might be adorned with gold, silver and precious stones and Emperor Aurelian (AD 215-275) is on record as disapproving of painted shoes which he believed to be effeminate. He

51

forbade the wearing of red shoes, mullaei, as well as white, yellow and green shoes. Shoes might also be turned up with a point; these types were known as 'bowed shoes'. The soccus was a plain shoe, large enough to wear over shoes or sandals, similar to a galosh.

Ladies' shoes could be a very expensive item of dress. They were generally white, although the wealthy wore them in a variety of colours such as black, red, purple, yellow and green. They were richly embellished with fringes and gold embroidery as well as pearls and precious stones. In later years they were worn not only by the rich but also by the poorer classes, so that by the beginning of the third century the Roman Emperor Heliogabalus (AD 204-222) issued a proclamation prohibiting such expensive shoes to any but the higher ranking women. Roman women wore the closed shoe or calceus and the solea and crepida in town as well as for country wear. They did not differ much from those of the men.

Socks or foot coverings made of wool or goat's hair and called udones, were worn by the Roman women; men did also wear them but this was thought to be effeminate.

Breeches or trousers were not worn by the Romans until the legionaries began to fight in colder climates. The Roman breeches were at first short and tight-fitting but later became looser and longer, sometimes reaching to the ankles.

The Romans sometimes wrapped their legs and thighs with bandages or rolls of cloth for warmth. This fashion was introduced by the infirm and was adopted by a few of the rich and effeminate (who also wore mufflers to keep their necks warm).

## JEWELLERY, MAKE-UP AND ACCESSORIES

In the austere days of the Republic, the wearing of jewellery was frowned upon, but in the Imperial age rings, bracelets, necklets and fibulae began to be more commonly worn by both sexes. Gold and precious stones were profusely used by the wealthy. Women also decorated themselves with pen-

*Roman boy wearing a bulla around his neck*

52

dants, anklets, fillets on their hair and earrings.

The monile, a special type of necklace, was also worn by men, but then the metal was usually twisted. It was given by the Romans to soldiers as a mark of honour and a reward for their bravery. Ring chains were also worn around the neck by men as well as women.

Rings were worn, gold rings being at first permitted to the Senators and Equites only. Later the legionary tribunes were also allowed to wear them. The common people wore iron rings unless they had been presented with a gold one for some deed of valour. Later it became more usual for everyone to wear gold, especially under the Emperors. Many rings were inlaid with precious stones or had sculptured designs.

The early Romans generally wore one ring only on the third finger of the left hand. Later on they could wear several rings on each finger although this was considered rather effeminate. Rings were used for specific purposes as well as for ornamentation: as tokens, as pledges and as signets. A plain iron ring given to a woman before marriage was regarded as a pledge of union. Rings were never worn in times of mourning.

Jewellery was also worn out of superstition, to act as a charm. Roman boys of noble birth wore a bulla of gold which hung from the neck; this was a hollow, round or heart shaped ball inside which was placed an amulet. The sons of the less well-off had their bulla made of leather.

Gloves were first invented to protect the hands of workers and they were sometimes made of leather. Gloves were more commonly worn among the Romans than among the Greeks. Some were made with fingers, others without so that they resembled mittens.

Roman women made extensive use of a variety of cosmetics, some of which were composed of white lead, vermilion and other substances which were very bad for the skin. Roman ladies had a great variety of salves, oils and hair dyes, kept in a toilet box divided into compartments for powders and paints.

The recipes for some lotions still survive: one for curing spots was made from birds' nests. Men also made use of cosmetics and even rubbed their skin with pumice stone to make it smoother.

MILITARY

A Roman legionary's armour would consist of a helmet, a cuirass or breastplate, and greaves.

Helmets (galeae) were at first made of leather, but later were of bronze, with cheek

*Iron helmet*

*Roman protective armour with metal plates over a leather tunic*

53

and neck guards, for extra protection. A coloured horse-hair crest was sometimes worn, but usually only for ceremonial purposes. The greaves (ocreae) worn by the Roman were similar to those of the Greeks, and consisted of two metal plates reaching from the knee to the instep, and fastened by clasps. The later Roman soldiers wore no greaves, but used sandals tied with strings or short boots laced and lined with animal skin.

Beneath his heavy body armour, a Roman soldier would wear a woollen corselet with wide sleeves reaching to just above the knee, and a focale or military scarf of the same material, which prevented the armour from chafing the skin. In the early days of the Republic a Greek type of corselet was worn, consisting of bronze plates, shaped to the body contours and secured by hinges at the sides and shoulders. Later, this type of cuirass was replaced by a chain-mail coat of Celtic origin, known as a lorica. A special type of lorica, called the lorica segmentata, was introduced during the Imperial period. The front and back plates were strengthened with iron hoops tied with tags and loops.

The earliest type of shield used by the Romans was light and round and was called a clipeus, usually made of bronze. Later the clipeus was abandoned in favour of a long, rectangular and convex shield, the scutum. It was made of wood covered with leather and reinforced with iron.

In the early days the hasta or thrusting spear was the chief weapon. However, during the last century of the Republic the pilum, or throwing spear, became universal amongst the legions. Every legionary would carry two pila, each about 2 m (6 ft 6 in.) long, and a gladius or short sword. As well as his weapons, a soldier would have to carry his own personal kit, which included not only bedding and cooking equipment, but also a spade and pickaxe for digging trenches when the unit set up camp.

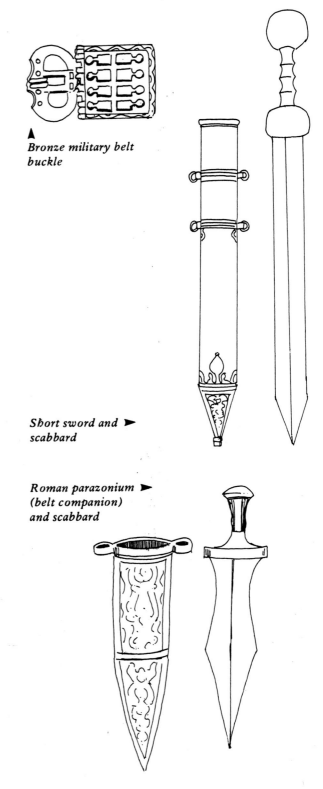

▲
*Bronze military belt buckle*

*Short sword and* ▶
*scabbard*

*Roman parazonium* ▶
*(belt companion) and scabbard*

# ANCIENT BRITAIN

ancient Briton.

The less civilised tribes that inhabited the interior and the north were generally just clothed in skins, ox skin being one of the more popular. Bear and sheepskin cloaks were common, depending on whether the people were herdsmen, shepherds or hunters. The cloaks were fastened by a thorn acting as a primitive type of brooch.

Women wore gowns that were long and flowing, with a belt. They could have long or short wide sleeves, or none at all. Gowns with long sleeves were sometimes worn beneath short sleeved over-tunics. Sometimes the skirt and top were separate, leaving a bare midriff. Sometimes the skirt, instead of being held up by a drawstring, might be worn with braces only.

By about the fourth century BC the people of southern Britain, more civilised than those in northern parts, had advanced from using fur as a covering and painting themselves with woad to wearing tunics and leg coverings made of coarse wool or flax, and fur or woollen mantles.

The men's tunics ended just above the knees and had either long or short sleeves. A strong belt which had a sword or dagger attached was also worn. For leg covering braccae were worn. These resembled trousers and were bound with criss-cross strips and held up at the waist by a drawstring. A kind of cape or cloak, usually made of fur, was worn over the tunic and fastened on the right shoulder.

Various kinds of cloth were manufactured in Gaul, made of fine wool dyed several different colours and spun into a yarn which was woven in stripes or checks. Both the Gauls and the Britons made their summer garments out of these materials which were the origin of the Scottish plaid or tartan and, indeed, apart from the plumed bonnet and the sporran, the full costume of a Highlander chief with trews, plaid, dirk and target or shield resembled that of a distinguished

## HEADWEAR AND HAIRSTYLES

There was very little headdress worn, shawls and capes being pulled over the head when necessary. Phrygian style caps similar to the Welsh national hat of today, were also occasionally seen.

*Typical hair fashion, with locks falling over the forehead, worn by Barbaric chieftain*

*Ancient Britons. The lady is in a long dress of Scottish plaid with a long cloak flung over her shoulders and fastened in the front with a brooch. The hair was worn long and loose. The man, a warrior, is in a short tartan tunic and carries a shield decorated with bosses in a circular design*

*Ancient British woollen cap* ➤

The Celts had long hair, either hanging loose or plaited, and the men wore long drooping moustaches.

*Early British shoe of cowhide drawn together by a string over the foot*
▼

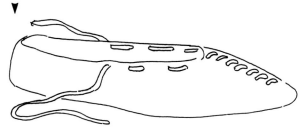

*Early British untanned leather shoe fastened with a leather thong beneath the heel and over the instep*
▼

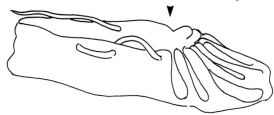

*Ancient British engraved brass torque*
▼

*Ancient British shield*
▼

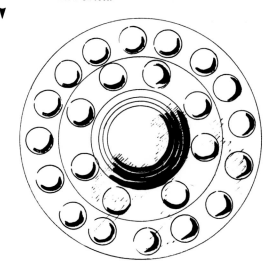

*Roman boot, later adopted by the Britons*
▼

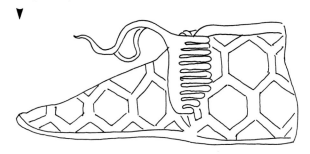

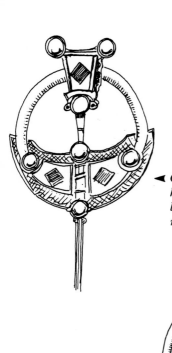

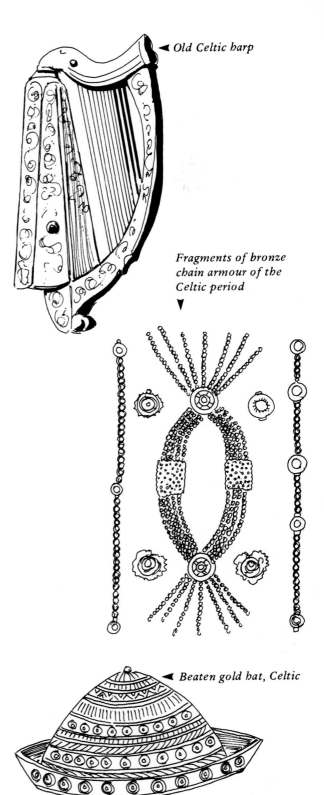

◄ Old Celtic harp

◄ Celtic pin with a heavy head made of inlaid bronze, worn by both men and women

Fragments of bronze chain armour of the Celtic period ▼

Inlaid bronze brooch, ► Celtic

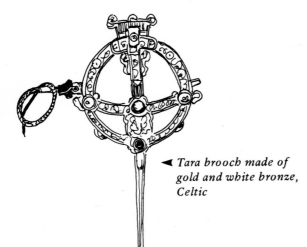

◄ Tara brooch made of gold and white bronze, Celtic

◄ Beaten gold hat, Celtic

Footwear for both men and women was made of untanned leather with fur inside. The sole and upper part was made in one piece fastened with thonging around the instep and ankles.

_____ JEWELLERY _____

Ornamentation consisted of rings, bracelets, armlets and collars or necklaces of twisted gold or silver wire. The necklaces were also known as torques. The Britons were so fond of these ornaments that those who could not afford them in precious metals wore them made of iron. Rings were generally worn on the middle finger. Another form of decoration was a breastplate or gorget. These breastplates were often made with highly embossed designs and were hollowed out at the neck.

_____ MILITARY _____

For battle the early Britons stripped off their clothes and stained their bodies with dyes in order to make themselves look fearsome. The most commonly used dye was woad, which was blue, although purple and scarlet dyes were also in use.

The first British peoples manufactured swords, spear blades and arrow heads from bronze. They were taught to make these by traders from Tyre, an important commercial city of antiquity on the Mediterranean. The lance head, made of a long bone ground to a point and inserted into a split at the end of a wooden shaft where it was secured by wooden pegs, was succeeded by a metal blade shaped similarly. Later, the shaft, instead of having the blade inserted, was fitted with a socket and, later still, the blade assumed a classical form. Arrows and hatchets also underwent gradual improvements from the earlier bone and flint types.

Swords may have been introduced into Britain by the Phoenicians. The hilt was usu-

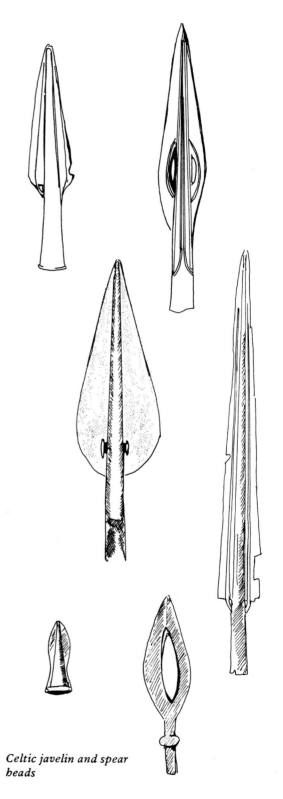

*Celtic javelin and spear heads*

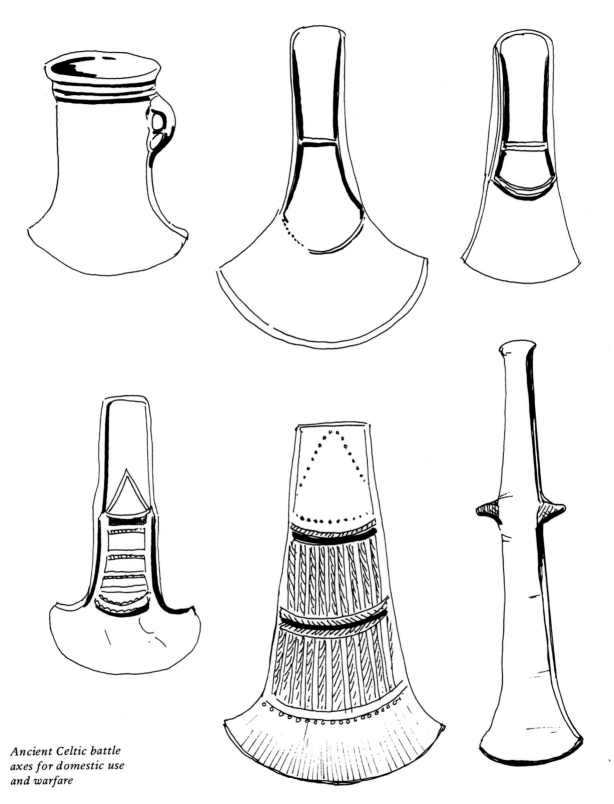

*Ancient Celtic battle axes for domestic use and warfare*

60

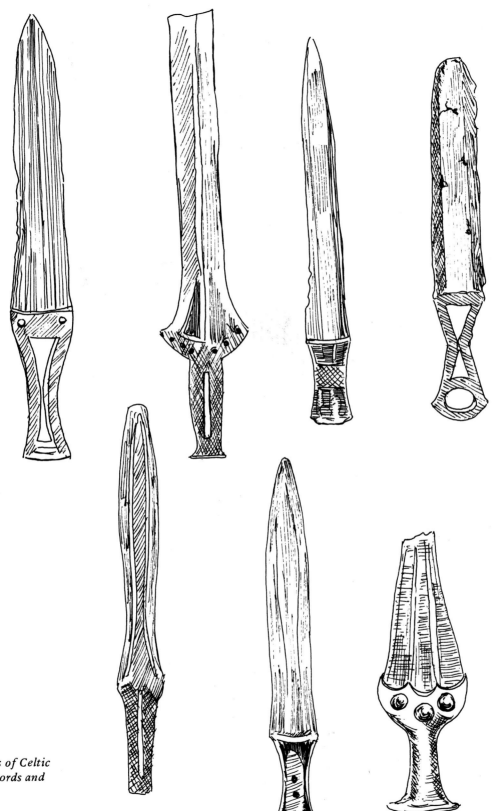

*Fragments of Celtic
bronze swords and
handles*

Celtic man with long
hair and a short tunic
belted at the waist. The
footwear is of untanned
leather fastened with
thonging to above the
ankles. The sword,
dagger and brooch are
all ornate

*Bone and kimmeridge coal necklace, Ancient British* ▲

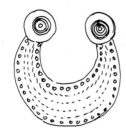

◀ *Druidal ornamented breastplate consisting of simple raised lines*

◀ *Druidal tiara ornamented with indented lines and zig-zags*

*Druidal ornament* ▶

ally made of horn and the blade, of bronze, had a very Eastern appearance. One unusual type of flat, circular shield was made of wicker. These were so ingeniously made that the Romans, once they had seen them in Britain, introduced them to Italy. The shields were faced with a thin plate of metal ornamented with concentric circles with small knobs between. They were about 60 cm (24 in.) in diameter with a hollow boss in the centre to admit the hand, as they were held at arm's length in action.

## CLERGY

The clergy were divided into three orders, the Druids, the Bards and the Ovates. The Druids wore white, the colour of truth and holiness, the Bards wore long, sky blue robes to represent peace, while the Ovates, whose profession was astronomy and medicine, wore green, the colour of learning and of nature. The disciples of these orders wore variegated dresses of the three colours, white, blue and green. Arch Druids or High Priests also wore an oak garland, sometimes surmounted by a gold tiara. The mantles could be fastened at the shoulders by being drawn through a ring which resembled a small bracelet.

63

# ROMAN BRITAIN

The Romans began to influence the Britons when they were active in Gaul during the first century BC, and after the conquest (43 AD) this influence became more apparent.

Under the Romans the Britons wore Celtic dress with adaptations, and there was a tendency to copy Roman fashions. The upper classes imported better quality wool and linen materials from Rome until manufacturing methods in Britain improved.

In AD 78, Julius Agricola became the governor of Britain and he encouraged the adoption of Roman ways and styles of dress. The braccae were abandoned by the Britons living in the east and south and the Roman type tunic, which reached the knees and was worn with a cloak or mantle became general wear for the better-off classes.

The Roman laena, a large rectangular woollen cloak, was worn in inclement weather. It was worn belted with part drawn over the head by the women. The sagum, a short cloak originally worn by Roman soldiers, was also adopted, and was usually blue or black.

Women's clothes altered very little in this period. Women generally wore two tunics, the lower one reaching the ankles while the over-tunic or gown, with elbow-length loose-fitting sleeves, reached half way down the thighs. A girdle was sometimes worn around the waist.

In the time of Boudica, Queen of the Iceni, a tribe of eastern Britain, women's dress consisted of tunics of several colours, falling in folds. These were worn under robes of coarser material which were fastened by a brooch or fibula. Hair was generally worn long and allowed to hang down over the shoulders.

Men's hair, although worn longer than that of the Romans, was slightly shorter than it has been prior to the Roman conquest. Jewellery came in a mixture of Celtic and Roman styles but as gold was not easily available, bronze, jet, enamel, bone and ivory were widely used.

## MILITARY

Military attire was similar to that of the Romans and consisted of the lorica or cuirass of chain-mail or leather strips, but the helmets were those of the Celts. The tops could be decorated with a bronze comb or a turned-down brim with horns either side.

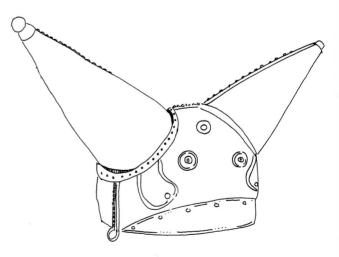

*Ornamental bronze helmet*

# GLOSSARY

| | |
|---|---|
| *Amulet* | Piece of jewellery worn around the neck as a lucky charm |
| *Anaxyrides* | Leg and thigh covering. Greek name for Persian style trousers |
| *Angustus Clavus* | Two narrow decorative bands worn by the Roman Knights on their tunics |
| *Baldrick* | Sword-belt worn from shoulder to opposite hip |
| *Baxea* | Type of Roman sandal, with soles of palm leaf |
| *Bodkin* | Bronze or bone hairpin (Greek or Roman). Pin used for fastening garments together (Saxon) |
| *Boss* | Circular metal ornamental knob or protuberance, usually on a shield or helmet |
| *Braccae* | Type of trousers hanging below the knees, sometimes down to the ankles, and tied |
| *Buckler* | Small shield |
| *Bulla* | Hollow ball worn around the neck |
| *Burnoose* | Long circular mantle with hood (Biblical) |
| *Buskin* | Type of boot |
| *Byrrus* | Woollen cloak with cowl (Roman) |
| *Calceus* | Shoe or half-boot, sometimes to calf height. Also worn by the military. The women's version was lighter and more elegant (Roman) |
| *Caliga* | Shoe or sandal with a thick nailed sole worn by Roman soldiers |
| *Campagus* | Type of sandal laced over the instep with a high piece of leather around the heel, worn by Roman soldiers |
| *Candys* | Tight-sleeved type of kaftan or mantle (Persian) |
| *Cappan* | Conical cap |
| *Caracalla* | Narrow tight-fitting garment with long sleeves and sometimes with a hood |
| *Chaplet* | Wreath or circlet for the head |
| *Chethomene* | Straight-sleeved ankle length girdled tunic (Jewish) |
| *Chignon* | Knot or coil of hair pinned to the head |
| *Chiton* | Greek tunic or undergarment |
| *Chlamys* | Greek rectangular mantle or cloak |
| *Chlandion* | Babylonian cloak |
| *Chlanis* | Light-weight cloak (Greek) |
| *Cidaris* | Tiara of the ancient Persian kings and Jewish high priests |
| *Clavus* | Vertical purple band decorating Roman tunics |
| *Cothurnos* | High Greek boot, laced up in front |
| *Cowl* | Hood attached to a cloak |
| *Crepida* | Roman sandal or bootee held on with thonging |
| *Cuirass* | Roman military corselet |
| *Cyclas* | Circular Roman cloak |
| *Dalmatica* | Roman wide-sleeved overgarment |
| *Diadem* | Crown |
| *Dirk* | Type of dagger |
| *Embas* | Greek laced shoe or boot |
| *Endromis* | Laced Greek boot worn by travellers |
| *Ephod* | Overgarment worn by Jewish priests |
| *Exomis* | Short sleeveless tunic with the right side open (Greek) |
| *Fibula* | Ornamental brooch or fastening similar to a safety pin |

66

| | |
|---|---|
| *Fillet* | Band tied around the head |
| *Focale* | Roman military scarf |
| *Galerus* | Round cap made of skin |
| *Gorget* | Neck or throat decoration |
| *Greave* | Shin armour |
| *Hauberk* | Shirt made of mail |
| *Himation* | Rectangular outer mantle draped in various ways (Greek) |
| *Hyke* | Cloak or mantle (Biblical) |
| *Infula* | Lappets, bands or pendants hanging from a mitre or other headwear |
| *Kaftan* | Overgarment with fitted back, the front usually left open |
| *Kalasiris* | Egyptian linen tunic covering the legs, sometimes pleated |
| *Kekryphalos* | Greek headscarf |
| *Klaft* | Linen headcloth (Egyptian) |
| *Knemis* | Greave (Greek) |
| *Kyne* | Greek leather bonnet or metal helmet |
| *Lacerna* | Type of mantle also serving as a bed covering when travelling, open in front and fastened with a brooch at the neckline |
| *Laena* | Roman cloak |
| *Latus Clavus* | Broad band decorating the tunic of the Senators |
| *Loincloth* | Band of material wound around the hips |
| *Lorica* | Armour of mail, leather or metal military corselet (Roman) |
| *Mitre* | Draped headdress, originally Persian |
| *Monile* | Necklace |
| *Mullaeus* | Red or violet shoe worn by Roman magistrates |
| *Ocrea* | Greave (Roman) |
| *Paenula* | Travelling cloak or mantle, also used as a bed covering (Roman) |
| *Palla* | Women's rectangular outer robe or mantle, sometimes open on one side |
| *Pallium* | Men's outer cloak, rectangular and sometimes open on one side |
| *Paludamentum* | Roman rectangular outer cloak with rounded corners |
| *Pectoral* | Jewelled or ornamental and decorative over-breastplate |
| *Peplos* | Loose gown worn over a Greek chiton |
| *Periscelides* | Greek anklets |
| *Perones* | Leather boots made of raw hide (Roman) |
| *Petasos* | Greek straw or felt hat with a flat crown and broad brim, tied with strings |
| *Phrygian cap* | Woollen coxcombed peaked cap with a turned-down point and cords fastening under the chin. Originated from the Persian mitre |
| *Pilos/Pileus* | Woollen cap, sometimes with a chin strap |
| *Quiver* | Case for holding arrows |
| *Sagum* | Soldier's cloak, Celtic and Roman |
| *Sandalium* | Sandal usually worn by women (Roman) |
| *Schenti* | Egyptian loincloth, passing between the legs |
| *Signet* | Seal |
| *Sisyra* | Thick mantle (Greek) |
| *Soccus* | Type of shoe or slipper worn by men and women in Greece but only by the women in Rome |
| *Solea* | Simple type of sandal with a wooden sole and a cord fastening (Roman) |
| *Stola* | Long loose overgarment worn by Roman women sometimes with two belts, one under the breast and the other at the hips |

| | |
|---|---|
| *Strophium* | Scarf-like belt wound around the body to support the breast (Roman) |
| *Synthesis* | Type of tunic worn at meals only (Roman) |
| *Tarentine* | White cloak of thin material (Greek) |
| *Theristrion* | Veil or light summer cloak for women (Greek) |
| *Tholia* | Wide brimmed hat with pointed crown worn by Greek women |
| *Thorax* | Chest armour or breastplate |
| *Tiara* | Head covering or crown held in place by a ribbon around the head |
| *Toga* | Civil attire of Roman citizens: plain piece of material draped leaving the right arm free |
| *Toga picta* | Toga of a fine cloth, usually purple with gold borders |
| *Toga praetexta* | Toga with a purple band |
| *Toga virilis* | Plain white toga |
| *Torque* | Circular necklace or armlet of wire, usually twisted |
| *Trabea* | Brocaded scarf worn by Roman Consuls |
| *Trews* | Celtic breeches and hose in one |
| *Tsitsith* | Blue tassels on Hebrew garments |
| *Tunica* | Type of Roman shirt |
| *Tunica recta* | Ungirdled garment worn by young women |
| *Tunica regilla* | Ungirdled tunic worn by women on their marriage |
| *Turban* | Eastern headdress consisting of a cap with a long piece of material folded in a criss-cross around it from the crown, the end being tucked into the folds |
| *Udones* | Full-length cloth stockings sewn together, fitting over the feet and worn to above the knees (Roman) |
| *Woad* | Blue dye |
| *Zona* | Broad flat girdle or belt worn by girls around the hips (Greek) |

Abrahams, Ethel B, *Greek Dress* John Murray 1908

Barfoot, Audrey, *Everyday Costume in England* Batsford 1961

Barton, Lucy, *Historic Costume for the Stage* A and C Black 1961

Black, J Anderson, and Garland, Madge, *History of Fashion* Orbis 1975

Boucher, Francois, *20,000 Years of Fashion* Abrams

Braun and Schneider, *Historic Costume in Pictures* Dover 1975

Bruhn W and Tilke, M, *Pictorial History of Costume* Zwemmer 1955

Cassin-Scott, J, *Costumes and Settings for Historical Plays I The Classical Period* Batsford 1979

*The Greek and Persian Wars 500-323 BC* Osprey 1977

Clinch, George, *English Costume from Prehistoric Times to the End of the 18th Century* Methuen 1909

Contini, Mila, *Fashion from Ancient Egypt to the Present Day* Hamlyn 1967

Gorsline, D, *What People Wore* Orbis 1978

Hansen, H H, *Costume Cavalcade,* Eyre Methuen 1960

Hope, Thomas, *Costumes of the Greeks and Romans* Dover 1962

Houston, Mary, G, *Technical History of Costume Vols 1 and 2* A and C Black 1954 and 1931

*Ancient Greek, Roman and Byzantine Costume* A and C Black 1954

Houston M G and Hornblower, F, *Ancient Egyptian, Assyrian and Persian Costume* A and C Black 1920

Kohler, Carl, *History of Costume* Dover 1963

Laver, James, *Costume* Cassell 1963

*Concise History of Costume* Thames and Hudson 1969

*Costume through the Ages* Thames and Hudson 1967

Lister, Margot, *Costume: An Illustrated Survey from Ancient Times to the 20th Century* Herbert Jenkins 1967

*Stage Costume* Herbert Jenkins 1954

de Montfauçon, Bernard, *Antiquitée expliquée et representée en Figures* F Delauline 1722

Pistolese and Horstig, *History of Fashions* Wiley 1970

Quennell, M and C H B, *Everyday Life in Homeric Greece* Batsford/Putnam 1930

Ruppert, Jaques, *Le Costume, Vol 1* Flammarion 1930

Saint-Laurent, Cecil, *History of Ladies' Underwear* Michael Joseph 1968

Selbie, R, *Anatomy of Costume* Mills and Boon 1977

Squire, G and Baynes, P, *Observers Book of European Costume* Warne 1975

| | | |
|---|---|---|
| Strutt, Joseph, | *Dress and Habits of the Peoples of England* | Henry G Bohn 1842 |
| Truman, N, | *Historic Costuming* | Pitman 1956 |
| Wilcox, R T, | *Dictionary of Costume* | Batsford 1971 |
| | *Mode in Costume* | Scribners 1948 |
| Wilkinson, | *Manners and Costumes of the Ancient Egyptians* | 1878 |
| Wilson, Lillian, | *The Roman Toga* | Johns Hopkins, 1924 |
| | *Clothing of the Ancient Romans* | Johns Hopkins 1938 |
| Yarwood, Doreen, | *English Costume from the 2nd Century to the Present Day* | Batsford 1972 |
| | *Encyclopaedia of World Costume* | Batsford 1978 |
| Kybalova, Ludmila, | *Pictorial Encyclopaedia of Fashion* | Hamlyn 1968 |
| | *Oxford Classical Dictionary* | Oxford University Press 1950 |